Make a
Chinese
New Year
Dragon

Conni Medina

Consultant

Timothy Rasinski, Ph.D.
Kent State University

Publishing Credits

Dona Herweck Rice, *Editor-in-Chief*
Lee Aucoin, *Creative Director*
Conni Medina, M.A.Ed., *Editorial Director*
Jamey Acosta, *Editor*
Robin Erickson, *Designer*
Stephanie Reid, *Photo Editor*
Rachelle Cracchiolo, M.S.Ed., *Publisher*

Based on writing from *TIME For Kids*.

TIME For Kids and the *TIME For Kids* logo are registered trademarks of TIME Inc. Used under license.

Teacher Created Materials

5301 Oceanus Drive
Huntington Beach, CA 92649-1030
http://www.tcmpub.com
ISBN 978-1-4333-3593-8
© 2012 by Teacher Created Materials, Inc.

Pop! Bang! See the bright colors. Hear the music. This is a Chinese New Year parade.

The dragon is the best part of the parade. It shakes its head and flips its tail.

You can make a dragon
to celebrate, too.

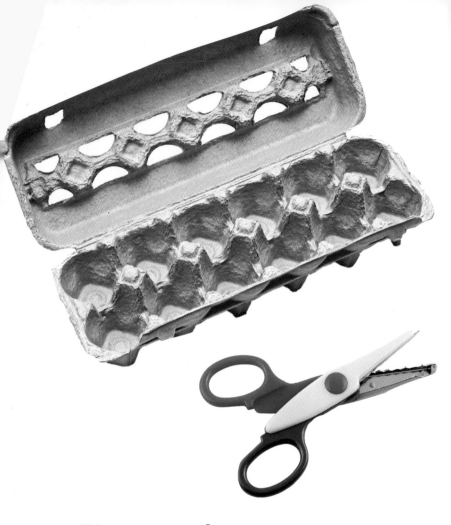

First, gather your supplies. You need an **egg carton** and **scissors**.

You need paint and brushes. You also need a **hole punch** and some red **ribbon**.

Are you ready to start?
Cut apart the egg carton
to make small cups for
the body.

Make your dragon as long as you like.

Paint the outside of the cups red.

Then add some spots or stripes. Your dragon should be colorful.

Use the hole punch to make two holes in each cup. The holes should be across from each other.

Choose one egg carton cup for the head and paint the inside black.

Add wiggle eyes and
pom-poms for extra fun!

Your dragon needs a
tongue. Cut a piece of red
ribbon and glue it inside
the mouth.

After the paint is dry,
glue the head to the body.

Then use the ribbon to tie
the dragon together.

You are ready for a
Chinese New Year parade!

Glossary

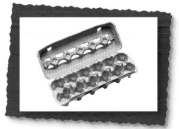

egg carton

hole punch

ribbon

scissors

Words to Know

bright

brushes

carton

celebrate

Chinese

colorful

gather

hole punch

mouth

music

paint

parade

piece

pom-poms

ribbon

scissors

stripes

supplies

tongue

wiggle